AMAZING HOCKEY STORIES

LEON DRAISAITL

Lorna Schultz Nicholson
Illustrations by D. A. Bishop

Scholastic Canada Ltd.
Toronto New York London Auckland Sydney
Mexico City New Delhi Hong Kong Buenos Aires

To all kids playing hockey, all over the world.
— *L.S.N.*

Scholastic Canada Ltd.
604 King Street West, Toronto, Ontario M5V 1E1, Canada

Scholastic Inc.
557 Broadway, New York, NY 10012, USA

Scholastic Australia Pty Limited
PO Box 579, Gosford, NSW 2250, Australia

Scholastic New Zealand Limited
Private Bag 94407, Botany, Manukau 2163, New Zealand

Scholastic Children's Books
1 London Bridge, London SE1 9BG, UK

www.scholastic.ca

Library and Archives Canada Cataloguing in Publication
Title: Leon Draisaitl / Lorna Schultz Nicholson ; illustrations by D.A. Bishop.
Names: Schultz Nicholson, Lorna, author. | Bishop, D. A. (David A.), illustrator.
Description: Series statement: Amazing hockey stories
Identifiers: Canadiana 20220496102 | ISBN 9781039700666 (softcover)
Subjects: LCSH: Draisaitl, Leon, 1995-—Juvenile literature. | LCSH: Hockey players—Germany—Biography—Juvenile literature. | LCGFT: Biographies.
Classification: LCC GV848.5.D69 S39 2023 | DDC j796.962092—dc23

Photos ©: cover: Mark Blinch/NHLI via Getty Images; cover background: Nik Merkulov/Shutterstock; 5: Jason Franson/The Canadian Press via AP; 6: Courtesy Draisaitl Family; 8: Courtesy Draisaitl Family; 15: Courtesy Prince Albert Raiders Hockey Club; 19: Matt Slocum/AP Photo; 25: Marissa Baecker/Getty Images; 33: Andy Devlin/NHLI via Getty Images; 36: Alexey Kudenko/Sputnik via AP; 41: Tony Avelar/AP Photo; 47: Marco Leipold/Alamy Stock Photos; 51: dpa picture alliance/Alamy Stock Photo; 52: Andy Devlin/NHLI via Getty Images; 57: Larry MacDougal via AP Photo; 64: Peter Schatz/Alamy Stock Photo.

Text copyright © 2023 by Lorna Schultz Nicholson
Illustrations copyright © 2023 Scholastic Canada Ltd.
All rights reserved.

No part of this publication may be reproduced or stored in a retrieval system, or transmitted in any form or by any means, electronic, mechanical, recording, or otherwise, without written permission of the publisher, Scholastic Canada Ltd., 604 King Street West, Toronto, Ontario M5V 1E1, Canada. In the case of photocopying or other reprographic copying, a licence must be obtained from Access Copyright (Canadian Copyright Licensing Agency), 69 Yonge Street, Suite 1100, Toronto, Ontario M5E 1K3 (1-800-893-5777).

6 5 4 3 2 1   Printed in China 62   23 24 25 26 27

CONTENTS

One-Percent Wonder 4

Early Years 6

Ups and Downs 18

    Down, Not Out 20

    Blast Off 28

Best Present Ever 32

    Hats Off 42

A Run for the Cup 54

    Giddy-Up! 58

ONE-PERCENT WONDER

Germany loves *fussball* — the German word for soccer — the way that Canadians love hockey. There are several professional soccer leagues, huge crowds for games and many superstar players. But there's another top athlete that's been stealing the spotlight in Germany, one who scores goals on the ice, not on the pitch.

Leon Draisaitl was born in Germany. Growing up there, his NHL dream might have seemed out of reach. Only about one percent of NHL players are German. It took determination, perseverance and sacrifice for Leon to make it to the top hockey league in the world. Of course, his blistering one-timer and a deep commitment to the players on his team helped, too! The work paid off and in 2020, Leon was the first German-born player to ever win the Hart Memorial Trophy.

In an interview after winning the coveted award, Leon talked about a very personal goal, saying, "It's a big honour. Our hockey is getting much better [in Germany] and we're producing more and more players. So hopefully this will somehow give little kids maybe some more joy of playing hockey and starting hockey instead of other sports. If I can help with that in any way, then I'd love to do that."

With his extraordinary skills, leadership abilities and commitment to teamwork, Leon has become an NHL superstar and his dream of raising the profile of hockey in Germany has become a reality.

LEON WAS NAMED AN ALTERNATE CAPTAIN FOR THE OILERS STARTING IN THE 2019-20 SEASON.

EARLY YEARS

Leon Tim Draisaitl was born in Cologne, Germany, on October 27, 1995. With its many gothic cathedrals, this 2,000-year-old city is considered a historic treasure. Hockey has been in Leon's blood since day one. His father, Peter Draisaitl, played for the German National Ice Hockey Team in three Winter Olympics. He also played in the 1996 World Cup in Montreal against NHL greats Mark Messier and Wayne Gretzky. When Leon was little, Peter played professionally for the Cologne Sharks, in the German hockey league. His mother often took Leon and his older sister, Kim, to watch their dad play.

LEON STILL TRAINS IN HIS HOMETOWN OF COLOGNE, WHERE HE FIRST PICKED UP A STICK AT AGE TWO.

SKATES OR CLEATS?

Leon started playing hockey in a league when he was five years old, but quit three years later to play soccer with his friends. He missed the fast-paced game on ice and returned to it when he was nine years old.

In Germany, kids play with a professional team's organization. Leon played in the Junior Cologne Sharks program. When he was twelve, the Sharks U16 team called him up. Leon played with boys who were three years older and much, much bigger! He held his own, scoring two goals and getting ten assists in ten games. The following year he made the U16 team from the start and quickly became a force. In the 30 regular season games, he scored 20 goals and earned 23 assists. Then in five playoff games, he scored a goal and earned six more assists.

Suddenly, Leon's skills were getting noticed. He wondered if he could become a professional player like his father. Or maybe even play in the NHL. There were hardly any German players in the NHL.

Leon and his dad, now a professional coach, discussed how Leon could best develop his game. The team in Mannheim was the strongest in the Schüler Junior League but . . . he'd have to move away from home.

LEON AND HIS FATHER WITH THEIR GAME FACES ON, OUTSIDE THE SHARKS' ARENA IN COLOGNE.

MOVING TO MANNHEIM

Leon was only 13 years old when his parents hugged him goodbye at a billet house in Mannheim, a city that which was hours away from his home in Cologne. The first night was hard. Leon was scared and missed his family. He sat in his room, worrying about how he was going to do. Two of Leon's new teammates, including Dominik Kahun, were also staying there, and Leon and Dominik quickly became friends. Leon felt a little less homesick.

In his first year with the Mannheim Young Eagles U16 team, Leon racked up the points. In 26 games, He earned 48 goals and 55 assists. His Eagles team won the Schüler-Bundesliga Meister Championship. This made them the best U16 team in Germany.

By the fall of 2010, Leon, now 15 years old, was taller and stronger. He found new length in his strides and his shot got harder. The German National U16 team asked Leon to play. He'd be facing off against other European national teams. When Leon put on his country's jersey for their first game that season, it felt different. Important. Leon proudly played in six games for Germany that year.

With his Mannheim team, Leon also started developing his leadership skills. He critiqued his own play after games — it was an easy way to improve. He wanted to help his teammates do the same, but it was hard to do without offending them. He watched older players who were good leaders, including future NHLer Tobias Rieder. Leon learned to deliver honest feedback in a way his teammates responded well to.

In his 2010–11 Mannheim season, Leon became a superstar. In 29 games, he scored 97 goals and earned 95 assists for 192 points! In five playoff games, he scored 16 goals and got 15 assists for 31 points. The Young Eagles won the Schüler-Bundesliga Meister Championship for the second year in a row. Leon had averaged an incredible six points a game in both the regular season and playoffs.

A BIGGER STAGE

Leon was so good that the coach of the Mannheim U18 team brought him up to play in six games after his U16 season was over. This was a big step. The U18 team played in the National Development League, and the next step up from that was the professional leagues. Leon played on this team for the next full season. Unlike his previous teams, the U18 team was sponsored and had more opportunities. They travelled to Finland, Sweden and even North America for tournaments.

Leon was also selected for the U17 German National Team. They travelled to Windsor, Ontario, for the 2012 World U17 Hockey Challenge. There were teams from Russia, the Czech Republic, Sweden and the USA. Team Canada competed with five teams made up of their best U17 players.

In the first two games, Germany didn't score a single goal, and they also lost their third and fourth games. But in their fifth one, they beat Canada's Team West 6–3! For Leon, the tournament was a chance to finally play the North American teams and to listen carefully to conversations about the Canadian junior leagues. He dreamed of playing in the NHL. These would be some of the players who were also trying to get there.

IN THE SPOTLIGHT

Leon was inspired for his 2012–13 season with the Young Eagles. In 35 regular season games, he had 21 goals and 35 assists, helping Mannheim to finish first in their division. They were headed to the Meister Championship, which ended in a best-of-three series against Berlin. Mannheim lost the first game, but won the second in their small home ice arena.

Usually, they had a few hundred fans at games. But for the final, they'd be playing in the big arena, where the pro team played. When Leon stepped on the ice, the crowd of 8,000 roared. Was this what the NHL was like? Leon scored twice and the Young Eagles won another championship.

Leon played in the IIHF U18 World Hockey Championship later that spring. The first game against Sweden was an 8–1 disaster. In the second game, Germany worked hard and beat Russia 4–2, with two assists for Leon. He picked up another two assists in a nail-biting 5–4 loss to Latvia. Leon's high point was the 6–2 win against Switzerland, where he potted two goals. Germany came third in their pool, advancing to the quarter-finals. Even though they lost to Finland, the German team improved . . . and the many scouts in attendance had noticed Leon.

THE IMPORT DRAFT

The Canadian Hockey League (CHL) has a yearly draft for European players, the Import Draft. Each of the 60 CHL teams is allowed two Europeans on their roster. In the 2012 Import Draft, there were 77 players — including Leon — from 11 European countries.

The Moncton Wildcats picked Russian player Ivan Barbashev. The Western Hockey League's (WHL) Prince Albert Raiders picked second. They had been keeping close tabs on Leon's international play and snapped up the six-foot German kid. The Raiders knew Leon had a great shot, fast passes and could protect the puck along the boards.

Back in Germany, Leon read online about being drafted. Unlike the NHL Draft, the Import Draft is not a live event. Did he even want to move? Finland and Sweden had expressed interest in him, and the NHL sometimes drafted players from the European leagues. Leon remembered the rough style of hockey from the young North American players he faced in the World U17 Hockey Challenge. He looked Prince Albert up on a map. Saskatchewan was very far away. Leon wanted to think about it.

While Leon was thinking, the Raiders' general manager, Bruno Campese, was doing whatever he could to convince him. Campese called Leon's dad, repeatedly, but Peter was away coaching in the Czech Republic. Campese knew that if he could just get one chance to talk to Leon and his dad, he'd be able to convince the young star to sign. Then, on a Friday night, Campese got an email. Leon and his dad would be in Cologne, but just for that weekend. Campese jumped on a flight and was in Germany the next day for lunch. Even though he was jet-lagged, he was thoroughly impressed by the teen, who asked such direct and intelligent questions. He assured Leon that playing for the Raiders would help him reach his ultimate goal: the NHL.

Leon agreed . . . but he was nervous.

HELLO, CANADA!

Leon arrived in Prince Albert in late August of 2012. It seemed like a good sign that NHL superstar Mike Modano had once stayed with Leon's billet.

At first, Leon found the language barrier hard. He was used to being able to use his sense of humour in the dressing room, but he didn't know enough English to be funny. No one laughed at his jokes! He signed up for an English class at the local high school, but the class was studying Shakespeare. Leon didn't think Shakespeare would help him joke around with his teammates. Instead, Leon learned English by watching television, movies and YouTube.

Leon would soon have a chance to speak German in the dressing room again, at the the 2013 IIHF U20 World Junior Hockey Championship. It was being held in Russia from December 26 to January 5. It was a tough tournament for Germany. They lost every game in the round robin — badly — with scores like 8–0 and 7–0. On the bright side, every game was a learning experience for the German team. Leon got a chance to play against top talents like Ryan Nugent-Hopkins and Nathan MacKinnon.

Leon returned to Prince Albert, finishing the 2012–13 season with 21 goals and 37 assists in 64 games. The Raiders made it to the playoffs but were beaten by the Red Deer Rebels 4–0 in the first round. Still, it was a decent rookie year considering he was getting used to the smaller North American ice surface. The game here was quicker. Leon learned to pass faster and get tougher along the boards.

At the end of April, Leon played for Germany in the 2013 IHF U18 World Championships in Russia. After a 9–1 loss to Sweden, they faced Canada and lost 3–1. At least the loss to the powerhouse Canadian team wasn't as bad as it could have been.

Then against Slovakia, Leon had a goal and four assists to help Germany win 6–3, and they made it to the quarter-finals! Germany ended up losing to Russia 8–4, but they had made improvements over the previous year. To help his country get further, Leon needed to work even harder.

On June 30th, Leon was glued to the television for the 2013 NHL Entry Draft. Nathan MacKinnon went first overall. Then, in the 13th spot, Raiders alternate captain, Josh Morrissey, was selected. Leon cheered for his teammate and set a goal — he would be drafted in the first round, too. To do that, he would need a spectacular 2013–14 season because his own draft was only a year away.

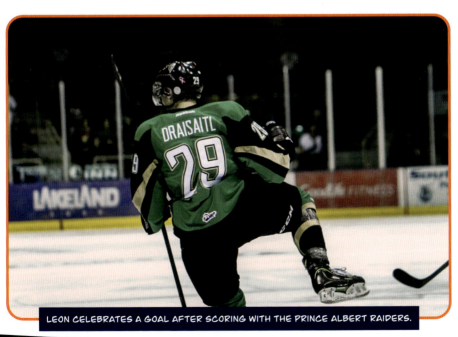

LEON CELEBRATES A GOAL AFTER SCORING WITH THE PRINCE ALBERT RAIDERS.

NEXT LEVEL

Leon's coaches knew how determined Leon was to take his game to the next level. And they couldn't help but notice how well he was able to work with his teammates, both on the ice and in the locker room. Leon was honest about what they needed to improve on, but was always fair and positive about how he put things. The coaches decided that Leon would start the 2013–14 season as alternate captain.

Leon played with intensity game after game and the points racked up. During games the announcers made comments such as: "Left circle, cut to the middle and Draisaitl scores!"; "Oh, what a move Draisaitl made to get the puck high!"; "Strong enough to outwork and outmanoeuvre"; and "Beautiful bank by Draisaitl."

In late December, Leon headed to Sweden to play for Germany in the 2014 IIHF World Junior U20 Hockey Championships. Germany lost their first game 7–2 to Canada. Leon played against Connor McDavid, who was then only 16. Leon noticed McDavid's speed and skill — everybody did! Unfortunately, Germany ended up in the relegation round where they faced Norway in a best of three. The losing country would drop to the B division. Leon was determined that would not be the outcome for Germany. After they lost the first game to Norway, Leon came out firing in the second, scoring two goals to take his team to a 4–3 win. Germany won the third and final game 3–1. Leon breathed a sigh of relief.

By the end of his Raiders season, Leon had racked up a phenomenal 105 points in 64 games. He'd scored 38 goals and picked up a whopping 67 assists. His performance helped them make the playoffs, but they lost their first-round series against the Edmonton Oil Kings 4–0. He wasn't ready to hang up his skates for the spring quite yet, however.

Leon was asked to play in the IIHF World Hockey Championships being played in Minsk, Belarus, that May. It was a huge opportunity to get noticed. The stands would be full of scouts and there were top NHL players competing in this tournament. Leon couldn't believe he was playing against NHL superstars like Johnny Gaudreau and Alexander Ovechkin. Germany won their first two games against Kazakhstan and Latvia, but went on to lose their next five games. Leon had scored one goal and earned three assists and was considered a standout player for Germany.

All in all, Leon had a great season. But would it be enough to reach his goal of being selected in the first round of the draft?

UPS AND DOWNS

Leon travelled from the World Championships to Toronto for the NHL Combine being held from May 26 to 31, 2014. He weighed in at 92.5 kilograms (204 pounds) and was 187 centimetres (6'2") in height. He didn't crack the top 10 in any of the physical contests, and he also wasn't sure how he fared in the interviews with the general managers. They'd asked a lot of questions, including "Would you rather be a pilot, a doctor or a sharpshooter?" Was that a trick question? Leon answered "doctor."

The 52nd NHL Entry Draft was a live event, held on June 27 and 28 at the Wells Fargo Center in Philadelphia, Pennsylvania. Unlike the Import Draft, it was a huge in-person event. Leon needed to buy a suit! Dressed in a black jacket, checkered tie, and crisp white shirt, he waited in the stands with his parents.

The Florida Panthers had the first pick. They chose defenceman Aaron Ekblad. Leon wasn't surprised; Ekblad had been talked about as the number one pick for months. The Buffalo Sabres had the next pick, calling forward Sam Reinhart. The Edmonton Oilers had the next pick. Leon sat nervously in his seat. It would be so great to be an Oiler. But Sam

Bennett, a forward for the Kingston Frontenacs, had been ahead of him in the rankings all year. Would it be Bennett?

Then the Oilers' general manager called Leon's name. He'd gone third in the first round. He was the highest-drafted German player ever! He hugged his family and headed to the stage. Leon proudly pulled on his blue-and-orange jersey.

On August 12, he signed a three-year, entry-level contract with Edmonton and was told to show up at training camp along with the other Oilers hopefuls.

AFTER THE DRAFT, LEON SAID HE HAD BEEN HOPING TO BE PICKED BY THE OILERS SO HE COULD WEAR THE JERSEY OF SUPERSTARS WAYNE GRETZKY AND MARK MESSIER.

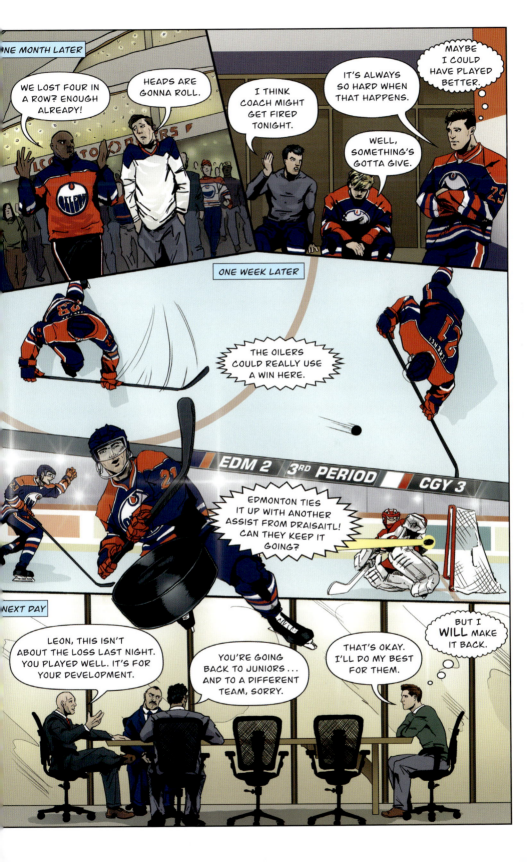

ON THE MOVE

Disappointed, Leon packed up his equipment and headed back to the WHL, this time to the Kelowna Rockets. On January 5, 2015, he walked into a new dressing room in his new jersey, his Oilers gear packed away. But that was okay — the Rockets were his team now. When he found out they didn't carry the type of stick that he used in the NHL, he switched. He wasn't going to ask for any special favours. Leon got to work, learning their plays right away.

Two days later, he took to the ice at Prospera Place in Kelowna for his debut with the Rockets, against the Vancouver Giants. A goal and an assist later, the Rockets won 4–2 and Leon picked up the game's first star. Maybe the sting of being sent down still hurt a little, but this was a good team. At this point in the season, the Rockets were first in their division.

The Rockets staff noticed right away that Leon was a true team player. Leon made connections quickly. If he and his teammates went out for a meal, he often offered to pay. Leon had saved up some of his NHL money and wanted to share with his new friends. He never complained, not even about riding a bus again after getting to fly on chartered flights as an NHLer.

After playing just 26 games for Kelowna, Leon had tallied 43 points, including 16 goals for the season.

The Rockets clinched the regular season title and the division title. They faced off against the Tri-City Americans in the first round of playoffs and won it in four straight games.

Kelowna won the next series against the Victoria Royals, 4–1. Next up, the Rockets faced the Portland Winterhawks. In just four games it was over . . . and the Rockets were the WHL Champions! Leon was the go-to player on the power play, scoring three short-handed goals.

Leon and the Rockets were headed to the 2015 Memorial Cup!

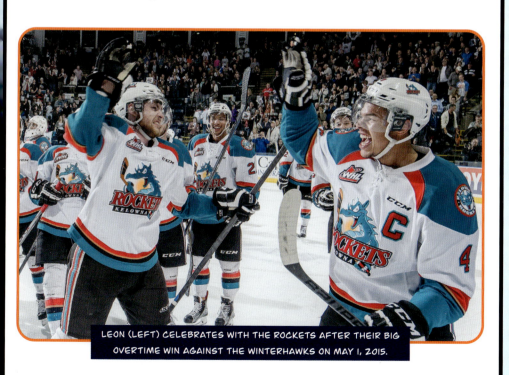

LEON (LEFT) CELEBRATES WITH THE ROCKETS AFTER THEIR BIG OVERTIME WIN AGAINST THE WINTERHAWKS ON MAY 1, 2015.

THE BATTLE BEGINS

The round-robin tournament took place in Quebec City from May 21 to 31. Vying for this prestigious cup were the Oshawa Generals, the Rimouski Océanic, the Quebec Remparts and the Kelowna Rockets. After the first round robin, the second place and third place teams competed to see who would meet in the final game against the team who had come first. The fourth-place team would go home.

Up first for the Rockets was the Remparts. The Remparts took an early 2–0 lead and an undisciplined Kelowna got more penalties than goals. The Remparts had been goading the Rockets, wanting them to fight. Leon stuck up for a teammate and got a misconduct. Halfway through the third he got back on the ice. In the dying minutes, Leon sunk a puck to the back of the net, making it 4–3 and getting the Rockets within a goal. They pulled their goalie and skated hard, but when the buzzer sounded, the Remparts had won. Leon felt terrible — this was not the way to help his team.

Before the next game against Rimouski, the Rockets coaches talked to their players about controlling their emotions and not letting the other team provoke them. Leon stepped on the ice with a different attitude. In the first minute, he set up a play for teammate Nick Merkley, who nailed it. The Rockets kept attacking. Leon put in a goal in the second period and one in the third! The Rockets won it 7–3 and Leon earned the third star of the game.

Leon was much happier with his game; he told Sportsnet: "It's nice to get everybody going, get a few guys on the scoresheet and show the world that we're better than we were against the Remparts."

The Rockets played Oshawa next and lost 2–1. Still, due to their high-scoring game against Rimouski, the Rockets came in second. Rimouski had the fewest points and was sent home. The Rockets would face the Remparts again in the semifinal game. If Kelowna won, they would play against the undefeated Oshawa Generals.

The first period started off fast and furious. Within seconds, tempers flared and players on both teams wound up in the penalty box. At the end of the first, it was tied 1–1 and the pressure was on.

> WHY DID LEON CHOOSE NUMBER 29?

> BEN THOMSON, STAR OF GERMANY'S RAVENSBURG TOWERSTARS, WORE IT. BEN USED TO HELP LEON PRACTISE HIS SHOTS.

BEST PRESENT EVER

Leon returned to the Oilers training camp in the fall of 2015. Connor McDavid, who had been drafted first overall in the 2015 NHL Entry Draft, was there, too. Leon desperately wanted to stay with the Oilers, and play with McDavid. Leon worked hard and had a decent pre-season. But as the Oilers home opener got closer, he got the bad news. He was going down to the American Hockey League to play for the Edmonton Oilers' farm team: the Bakersfield Condors. Dejected, Leon cleaned out his stall and left for yet another new dressing room.

Leon's first few games felt good, but the puck was finding different ways to stay out of the net. He was averaging five scoring chances in each game, but after six games, he had only one goal and one assist. How was he ever going to get called back to the NHL?

Leon turned 20 on October 27, 2015 . . . and got the best present ever. He was recalled to the Oilers for the game on October 29 against the Montreal Canadiens. This was his chance!

Suiting up back in the Oilers dressing room, Leon told himself that this time it was for keeps. He was going to stay in the NHL. But the game didn't start off with the bang that Leon was hoping for. By the end of the first period, the score was grim, 3–0 for Montreal. The mood in the dressing room was solemn. The Oilers came playing hard in the second period, but the score didn't budge. The period was winding down when there was a scramble in front of the net. The puck was fired over Canadiens goalie Carey Price's head and landed right on Leon's stick at an awkward angle. Leon immediately shot it right back at Price. It looked like it was in, but a Montreal defenceman, who was standing in the crease, batted at it and Price quickly covered it up. It went to review . . . and the ref called it a goal! The Edmonton bench cheered for Leon, even if it wasn't the prettiest goal.

LEON TAKES A SHOT ON MONTREAL'S CAREY PRICE DURING THE OCTOBER 29, 2015, GAME.

Edmonton came out flying in the third, and by the halfway mark, they'd tied the game. With less than a minute to play, Taylor Hall passed to Ryan Nugent-Hopkins, who fired it to Leon. In a perfect one-timer, it flew and found the back of the net. Leon's teammates jumped on him. He had two goals in the 4–3 victory, including the game winner, and earned the first star of the game.

BIG MOMENTS

On Halloween the Oilers played the Flames, their biggest rivals. After 40 minutes, the score was 4–2 for the Flames. The Oilers scored early in the third period. Shortly after, Leon sped down the ice. Taylor Hall fired him a pass and Leon one-timed it to tie the game! Unfortunately, the Flames scored with nine seconds left. It was all tricks, no treats for the Oilers.

But it was the November 3 game against the Philadelphia Flyers that was truly scary. Connor McDavid got smashed into the boards and broke his collarbone. The whole team was worried, and it was hard to play. Leon still managed to get two assists and the Oilers won it 4–2. In a post-game interview, a reporter asked him if McDavid's injury might open a door for him. Leon said, "It's an injury and this is a team sport. You don't want that to happen to anybody. Doesn't matter if a spot opens up or not."

Leon played well and stayed put, even after McDavid returned in February. The Oilers' last game of the season, on April 6, 2016, was also the last game to be held in the Rexall Place arena. There was a ceremony that included hockey legends Wayne Gretzky, Paul Coffey and Mark Messier. The Edmonton Symphony Orchestra played live as they introduced the players for the game that night and local legend Joey Moss carried out the banner. The Oilers bested the Vancouver Canucks that night, winning 6–2. Sadly, they were short of making the playoffs, but Leon could hold his head high. He had earned 19 goals and 32 assists in 72 games, coming second in scoring for the Oilers, behind Taylor Hall.

> WHAT'S LEON'S NICKNAME?

> HE HAS A FEW: THE DEUTSCHLAND DANGLER, NEON LEON AND THE GERMAN GRETZKY.

Leon and a couple of his Oilers teammates were still chasing a win, however. They were off to Saint Petersburg, Russia, to play at the IIHF World Hockey Championships. Connor McDavid and Taylor Hall were suiting up for Canada, and Leon for Germany.

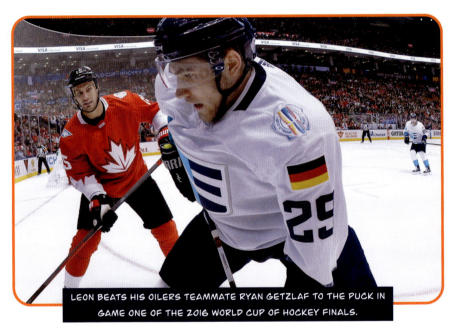

LEON BEATS HIS OILERS TEAMMATE RYAN GETZLAF TO THE PUCK IN GAME ONE OF THE 2016 WORLD CUP OF HOCKEY FINALS.

Germany's first game went to a shootout. Leon got the nod to take the first shot, but the French goalie made the save and Germany lost. They also lost to Finland, but they picked up a win against Slovakia. Then Leon had to play against his Oilers teammates instead of with them. Germany lost to Canada, 5–2. Next up was a win against Belarus, and then a big win against the USA. Germany scored with just

33 seconds left — a huge upset. With another win against Hungary, Germany came third in their pool and made the playoff round. They lost to Russia in the quarter-finals, but this was the best they'd ever done! Leon was proud of their progress.

In September, the World Cup of Hockey was being played in Toronto. Leon was asked to be on Team Europe, a big honour. They made it into the gold-medal round to play Team Canada in a best-of-three series. Team Europe lost two hard-fought games.

LET'S DO THIS!

The October 12, 2016, season opener was a big one for the Oilers. It would be Battle of Alberta *and* the first game in the new Rogers Place arena. Edmonton fans packed the stands for the music-and-light-filled grand opening. On Leon's first shift of the game, he lined up in the Calgary zone for the faceoff. The Flames got the puck and Leon raced forward, anticipating Calgary would be heading down the ice. When the Flames tried to clear the puck, Leon nabbed it just inside the blue line. He blasted a shot and teammate Patrick Maroon tipped it into the net. It was the first goal in Rogers Place and the crowd went wild! Edmonton went on to win 7–4. They won the next game in Calgary 5–3. Edmonton then won five of their next six games — a great start.

Over the up-and-down season the team was gelling. Leon played on different lines, but when he played with McDavid, they were often compared to Sidney Crosby and Evgeni Malkin of the Pittsburgh Penguins. And by the end of the season, the Oilers were more up than down. McDavid won the Art Ross Trophy with 100 points. Leon was second in the Oilers' scoring race with a healthy 29 goals, 48 assists and 77 points. Even better, the Oilers were headed to the playoffs for the first time in 11 years!

ORANGE CRUSH

On April 12, 2017, Leon looked out at the crowd in awe as he stepped onto the ice for game one of the first round of the playoffs. The stands were a sea of orange. Fans were waving pompoms and cheering loudly. The atmosphere was electric! The Oilers took an early 2–0 lead, but the San Jose Sharks came back with one goal in the second period and another in the third to take the game to overtime. The Sharks scored in the first four minutes of OT to win it.

Leon used his playoff experience with Kelowna to shrug off the loss. In game two, still on home ice, the

Oilers won 2–0. Game three in San Jose was another low-scoring affair, but Edmonton took it 1–0. Up 2–1 in the series, no one was ready for what happened next . . . the Oilers lost 7–0, a crushing blow. Many media pundits said Edmonton could not come back from such a horrible loss. But inside the dressing room, Leon and his teammates felt differently.

The next game was back in Edmonton. Stepping on the ice, Leon heard the roaring crowd. The Oilers hit the post four times before Patrick Maroon scored. But then the Sharks hit a stride and took a 3–1 lead. Late in the second, Leon was in the Sharks' end. He dangled around a defenceman and saw teammate Mark Letestu in the slot. Leon passed the puck through Sharks' legs and skates, putting it right on Letestu's stick. Letestu made the shot, and it was 3–2. When the Oilers tied it up at 17:14 in the third period, the fans were so loud Leon couldn't hear his teammates talk. The game was going to overtime. Would it be like game one all over again?

DOES LEON HAVE PETS?

LEON HAS A DOG NAMED BOWIE. BOWIE'S NICKNAME IS BOBO.

Early in the OT period, Leon blasted a bullet of a shot that hit the post. The battle went up and down the ice. Then Leon saw a loose puck. He raced toward it. Skating over the blue line, he saw McDavid with him. They flew on a two-on-one rush. Leon fired a pass to McDavid, who rifled a shot, but the Sharks goalie made the save of the game. The minutes ticked by. With less than two left in the period, Leon skated down the wing, stopped, stickhandled and fired off a pass from a right corner angle to Oilers centre David Desharnais, who one-timed it into the net. They won and were now up 3–2 in the series.

Game six was back in San Jose, and the Oilers were keen to win it there. But a few Edmonton players had the flu and weren't feeling well, including Leon. A tense first period was scoreless. But less than a minute into the second, Leon picked up a pass from Edmonton defenceman Adam Larsson and took off on a breakaway. Leon's long strides got through the Sharks' defence, and he fired the puck through the five-hole. Less than a minute later, Leon's teammate Anton Slepyshev scored on a breakaway. They were up 2–0. But in the third period, the Sharks scored. Could the Oilers hold their lead? With seconds left on the clock, McDavid fired the puck into San Jose's net. They were on to round two!

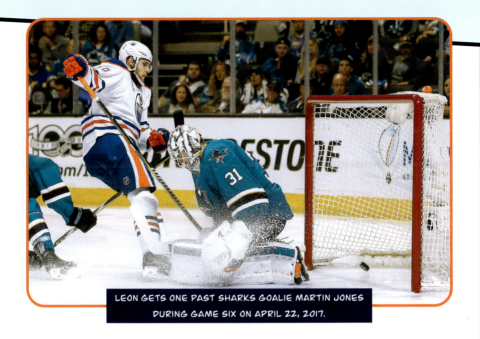

LEON GETS ONE PAST SHARKS GOALIE MARTIN JONES DURING GAME SIX ON APRIL 22, 2017.

Leon was hyped for the second round — the whole team was. They'd be facing the Anaheim Ducks, who they'd had decent success against during the regular season. Edmonton won the first game 5–3. Leon picked up mega points with three assists and a goal. He made Oilers fans dance in the streets. Edmonton also won their second game in Anaheim. The team was feeling great coming back to home ice, but then they lost the next two games. The series was tied 2–2 and heading back to Anaheim. Could the Oilers get their momentum back?

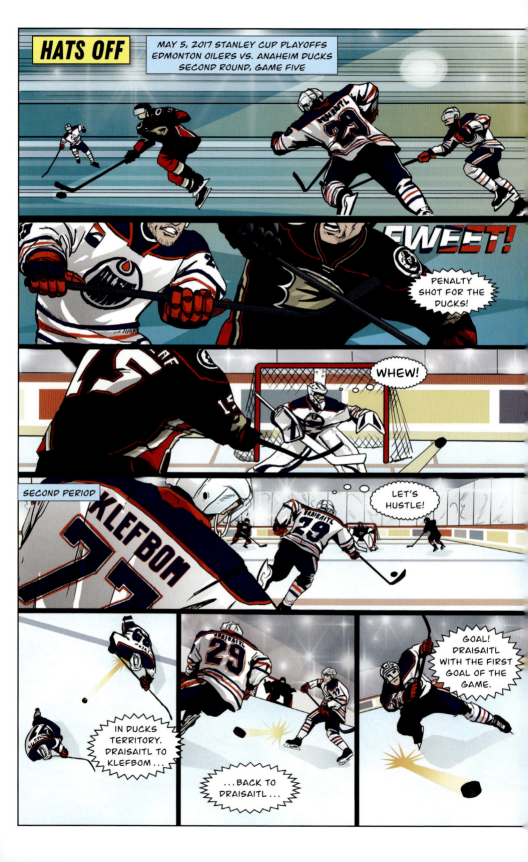

HAT TRICKS AND HOMETOWNS

Leon's hat trick got Edmonton to game seven, to be played in Anaheim on May 10, 2017. The Oilers opened the scoring, but the Ducks came flying back, outshooting the Oilers and making it 2–1 by the third period. Although the Oilers battled to the dying minutes of the game, they couldn't get that one last goal in. It was a huge disappointment, but Leon had learned a great deal from his first taste of NHL playoff action.

But he wasn't ready for summer vacation quite yet. The 2017 IIHF World Hockey Championship was taking place in Germany. And not only in Leon's home country, but in his hometown, Cologne! When he got there, the tournament was already under way, but he was still in time to play in Germany's last two games.

Back on the big ice surface, Leon helped his team make it to the quarter-finals where they were to face the talented Canadian team. Germany lost 2–1, but it still felt like a victory to Leon. His team played hard and the score was close. There were lots of German kids watching, cheering and asking for autographs. Leon did every interview he was asked to do. He wanted to showcase hockey in Germany in any way he could. It was almost better than winning.

LEON (FAR RIGHT) USUALLY SUITS UP WITH OILERS TEAMMATES (LEFT TO RIGHT): RYAN NUGENT-HOPKINS, DARNELL NURSE AND CONNOR McDAVID.

GREAT EXPECTATIONS

Hopes were high at the start of the 2017–18 season for Leon and the Oilers. Reporters made predictions on whether he and McDavid would play on a line together again. Leon ignored the fuss and focused on the October 4 season opener instead. It turned out to be a shutout against Calgary, with McDavid scoring all three of the goals and Leon getting two assists.

It would be another season of highs and lows. A December four-game winning streak was followed by four losses. In February, they had a six-game losing streak. The Oilers failed to secure a playoff spot. But there were some bright spots. Leon improved his stats, finishing second in the team scoring race with 25 goals and 45 assists for 70 points. Linemate

McDavid finished with 108 points, winning the Art Ross Trophy again. Could Leon ever win that trophy? Maybe, but he had some ground to make up first.

The 2018–19 season was tough. After losing six out of seven games in November, the Oilers head coach was fired. Leon knew this was part of pro hockey, but it still made him sad. His father had been fired before and Leon remembered how hard it had been for his family. Then in January, after another losing streak, the general manager was also let go.

With so many changes it was hard for the team to have that "gelled" feeling. Discouragingly, they came second-last in the Western Conference, but Leon still managed to hit a big milestone. He'd scored 50 goals, and with his 55 assists, he'd earned 105 points — his first time with NHL totals over 100. Maybe the Art Ross Trophy wasn't out of the question someday!

In May, Leon headed to Slovakia for the 2019 IIHF World Hockey Championships. The Germans started out strong, with wins over Great Britain, Denmark, France and Slovakia. Next up Germany faced the powerhouse Canadian team, which included Leon's good friend and Oilers teammate Darnell Nurse. Germany lost 8–1, and then lost to the USA 3–1. But in their last round-robin game, Germany won against Finland, who went on to win the tournament, beating the Canadian team for the gold. It was considered Germany's best performance at the championships. Leon helped them get there, playing all eight games, with five goals and three assists.

WHERE DOES LEON LIKE TO CHILL?

WHEN HE'S NOT ON THE ICE, LEON LIKES TO RELAX IN MAJORCA, SPAIN.

BIG LOSSES AND BIG WINS

After the poor 2018–19 season, hopes weren't high for Edmonton's next one. But Leon got to start it with a bit of good news. He and Darnell Nurse were made assistant captains. Leon was determined to help his team play better. He knew he could help motivate his teammates in the dressing room as well as be a playmaker on the ice. In the 2019–20 season opener against the Flames, played on October 2, Leon opened the scoring with a quick one-timer from the side of the net. With his goal and two assists, the Oilers bested the Flames 3–2, and went on to win the next five straight games.

Leon kept up the pace. The Oilers were having their best season in years . . . until it all came to an abrupt halt on March 13, 2020, when the COVID-19 pandemic ended the regular season. By this point, Leon had already earned a whopping 110 points — 43 goals and 67 assists in 71 games to lead the entire league in scoring. Pandemic or not, Leon's amazing performance won him the Art Ross Trophy!

But when the shortened playoff tournament began in August, the Oilers shockingly lost their qualifying round series against the Chicago Blackhawks. Leon couldn't understand what had happened to his team. They had lost all their momentum.

But at the NHL Awards, Leon was so happy and proud to win both the Ted Lindsay Award and the coveted Hart Memorial Trophy. He told the NHL News, "You dream of these things, no question, but until you do it, it seems so far away. I'm proud in a way, of course, but I know that I still have lots of things to work on. There's many things in my game I can improve and I am looking to do that every year."

But another big award was still to come. Leon was stunned and humbled when he was chosen as the 2020 German Sportsman of the Year. This honour was usually awarded to athletes who played individual sports: skiing, swimming, tennis, track and field, even car racing. Leon was the first hockey player to win, in recognition for his years playing for Germany and his amazing performance in the NHL.

LEON ACCEPTING GERMANY'S SPORTSMAN OF THE YEAR AWARD, AS VOTED BY THE NATION'S MEDIA.

With the pandemic still affecting things, the NHL's 2020–21 season started on January 13, 2021. The teams split into two divisions — North and South. In the shortened 56-game season, Leon scored 31 goals and earned 53 assists for 84 points. Edmonton came second in the North Division, just after the Leafs. In the first round of the playoff action in May, the Oilers faced the Winnipeg Jets, a team they had easily beaten all season. Much to everyone's surprise, Edmonton lost four straight games. Leon was devastated — they were so much better than that.

THE DYNAMIC DUO

Leon was thrilled to hear the news for the start of the 2021–22 season. Fans would be allowed back in Rogers Place! It had been hard for the team to keep the energy up in an empty building. Leon had found the silence almost eerie.

The roar of fans got Leon's blood pumping. He had four assists in the Oilers' first two wins, against the Canucks and the Flames. In the third game of the season, against the Ducks, Leon picked up two goals and two assists. Already, he had eight points and the Oilers won nine of their first 10 games. They bumped around with wins and losses right through until Christmas. Leon was playing well, especially with McDavid on the power play. They earned the nickname "The Dynamic Duo."

LEON SCORES THE GAME-WINNING GOAL IN OVERTIME WITH AN ASSIST BY McDAVID IN THE OCTOBER 24, 2019 GAME AGAINST THE CAPITALS.

But then in December, the Oilers lost most of their games. Leon was battling the best he could. They had playoff potential — why were they losing? Tensions were high, and then in February, the Oilers changed up their coaching again. Leon was sad to see a coach get fired, but the change seemed to work. The Oilers won five games in a row. Leon kept racking up points. Jay Woodcroft, the new coach, liked putting Leon and McDavid together and it was fun for both of them. The Dynamic Duo were the backbone of the wins.

Leon improved many aspects of his game, especially defence. If the Oilers were on a five-against-three penalty kill, he was put on the ice — his long reach could bat the puck to stop a scoring chance. He also set a new franchise record with 24 power-play goals, blasting past Wayne Gretzky and Ryan Smyth, who had held the previous record of 20. He scored 55 goals — his most ever! — and tied his best points total of 110.

Leon was happy about his records, but he was more thrilled that his team had made the playoffs. The mood in the dressing room was upbeat, and it was great to see all his teammates so excited. Up first were the Los Angeles Kings. During the regular season, the Oilers were 3–1 against the Kings.

A RUN FOR THE CUP

Game one was held on May 2, 2022, on home ice. It had been five years since the Oilers had seen playoff action. Fans filled the seats. At the end of the first period, it was 2–1 for Los Angeles. Edmonton tied it up on a power play in the second period, then the Kings came right back. When the Oilers got another power play, Leon hit the ice. In a battle in front of the net, a Kings player broke a stick. McDavid picked up the puck and shot it to Leon. The puck hit the broken stick, but Leon nabbed it, stickhandled past the defence and tied the game. Unfortunately, the Kings scored in the last period to win.

The negative comments started immediately — the Oilers were going to lose. Leon stayed positive. Fired up, Leon and his Oilers won the next game with a decisive 6–0. In a shocker, the Oilers won the next game 8–2. But the next two wins were for the Kings. Now critics said the Oilers didn't have the emotional capacity to win. Game five was 3–1 for the Kings up until the third period. Edmonton scored but Los Angeles came right back. The Oilers took a penalty. Leon went out for the penalty kill. When the Kings got caught too deep, Leon grabbed the puck, raced down the ice . . . and scored short-handed! Then and a half minutes later, he scored a power-play goal to tie the game. Sadly, the Oilers lost in overtime. The Kings had a 3–2 series lead.

Game six was critical. In the first period, Leon got caught in a scrum in front of the net. He was wrestled to the ice by a Kings player. When Leon got up, he limped to the bench. Something wasn't right. But Leon ignored the pain and kept playing. Midway through the third period, it was tied at two each, when Leon saucer-passed the puck to his defenceman, Tyson Barrie, who took a slapshot and scored. The Oilers won the game 4–2 and were still in the run for the Stanley Cup.

But maybe Leon wouldn't be. He had a high ankle sprain. The team doctors told Leon that if he could manage the pain, his injury wouldn't get worse from playing. It also wouldn't get any better. That was all Leon needed to hear. Before the deciding game, the trainers taped his ankle tightly and gave him medication so he could play. The Oilers won 2–0, advancing to face the Flames in the second round. Leon was dying to play!

WHAT DOES LEON CALL HIS STICK?

THE BURGER FLIPPER!

A BIG BATTLE FOR ALBERTA

The Battle for Alberta did not disappoint the Oilers fans. It had all the ups and downs, hard hits, funny bounces, and goals called back. Game one started with a bang for Calgary, who scored two goals in under a minute, then another one five minutes later. The Oilers changed up their goalie and managed a goal. In the second period, the Flames immediately scored another two goals. It was 5–1! But then in a wild flurry of goals, Edmonton scored four times and the Flames once more. In the third period, the Oilers scored right away and the fans went wild. Edmonton had come back from a 5–1 game to make it 6–6! Then the Flames took control and scored three more times. The final score was 9–6, an incredible 14 goals in a single playoff game — though it was not good news for the Oilers.

In game two, the Flames opened each of the first two periods with quick goals. The Oilers answered back both times to tie it up. After regrouping during intermission, the Oilers scored to open the third period. Finally they were in the lead! Leon played hard even though his ankle ached. Late in the third, he saw a loose puck. He beat the Flames' defenceman, and with a deke and a quick release, he nailed it. At the buzzer it was 5–3 for the Oilers.

LEON SCORES A GOAL AGAINST FLAMES GOALIE JACOB MARKSTROM IN GAME TWO, PLAYED ON MAY 20, 2022.

Game three started with a scoreless first period. Then Leon set up teammate Zach Hyman, who sunk it, giving the Oilers a 1–0 lead. Evander Kane scored the next three for Edmonton. Leon had a big assist each time in the thrilling hat trick. The game ended 4–1 for the Oilers. Leon had an assist on every goal.

Back on home ice, the Oilers opened the scoring in game four. On the next power play, Leon gave a crisp pass to McDavid, who gave it to Hyman, who scored! Leon's assists kept tallying up as he got one on the next goal, too. The Oilers went to the dressing room with a 3–0 lead. But the Flames clawed back and scored two goals in the second and one in the third to tie the game. With only four minutes to go, the Oilers scored! They were up 3–1 in the series . . . and headed back to Calgary.

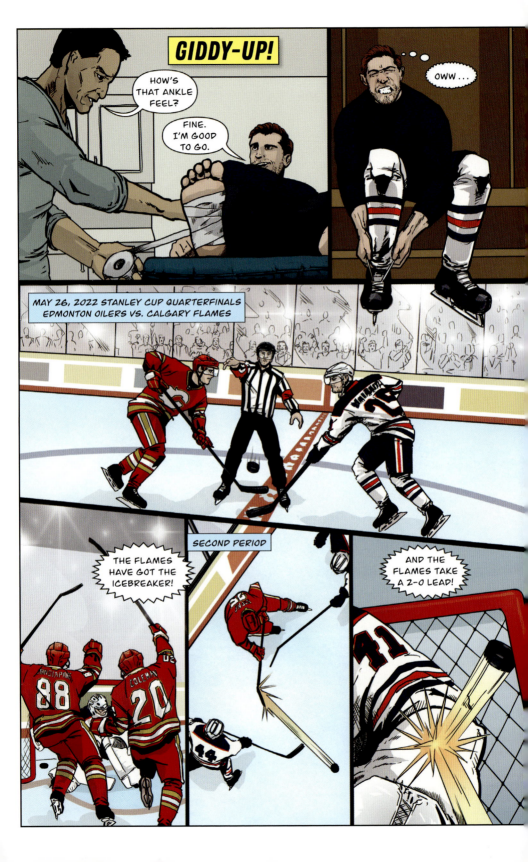

The Oilers were heading to the conference final against the heavily favoured Colorado Avalanche. Leon cringed every time he laced up his skate. He couldn't take his one-timer on the power play because he couldn't put weight on his right foot. Without Leon and a few of his teammates playing at full health, the Oilers lost 4–0. The Avalanche went on to win the Stanley Cup.

Still, Leon had hit some milestones during the playoffs. He scored seven goals and had 25 assists in 16 playoff games. In game five of the Battle of Alberta, Leon had picked up an assist that gave him 50 career playoff points in 33 games. This was the fourth-fastest in NHL history, behind only Wayne Gretzky, Barry Pederson and Mario Lemieux.

WHAT'S LEON'S FAVOURITE ADVICE FOR KIDS?

TRY NOT TO GET DISCOURAGED BY A BAD HOUR OR A BAD DAY. THIS, TOO, SHALL PASS!

KID AT HEART

Leon has a shelf full of awards and trophies, and international recognition of his talent. In his home country of Germany, he has broken long-standing records and raised the profile of hockey, something he dreamed of doing. And he's not done yet!

After each of his playing seasons wraps up, Leon always heads home to Cologne to visit with his family. He looks forward to having his favourites at family dinners: schnitzel with potato salad and his mom's homemade pasta bolognese. It's not quite a vacation, though. Leon is still working hard to promote hockey in Germany. When he's there, he does all the interviews he can. Leon uses his celebrity status to help not-for-profit organizations raise money and awareness for various causes, especially for ones that help underprivileged kids. He always makes time to attend local games and connect with kids face to face. Young players and fans crowd around him, asking questions, hoping for an autograph . . . and they often get one! Leon seems to enjoy that as much as the kids do.

On October 29, 2022, just before a Battle of Alberta game, Leon spotted a 15 year-old boy in the mostly Canadian crowd. The boy had a sign that was written in German. It said: "I came from Germany to see you!" After the pre-game warm-up, Leon skated over to say hello. They chatted for a minute in German, then Leon passed an autographed stick over the glass. The boy was thrilled, but between the two, it was hard to tell whose smile was bigger.

The only thing that might make Leon smile more would be to win a Stanley Cup. And if he keeps playing the sort of game he is famous for — helping teammates with their big shots and making goalies cringe with his own — Leon might add that to his trophy shelf, too.

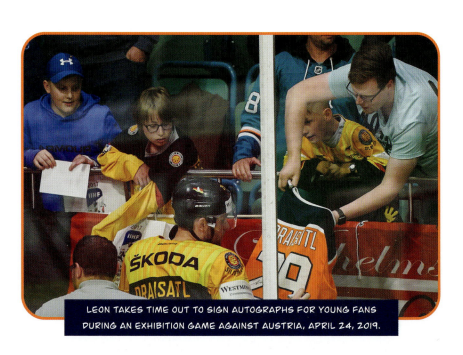

LEON TAKES TIME OUT TO SIGN AUTOGRAPHS FOR YOUNG FANS DURING AN EXHIBITION GAME AGAINST AUSTRIA, APRIL 24, 2019.